HEROES

Colin Powell

Other books in the Today's Heroes Series

★ TODAY'S ★ HEROES

Colin Powell

Gregg & Deborah Shaw Lewis

Zonderkidz

Today's Heroes: Colin Powell
Copyright © 2002 by Gregg and Deborah Shaw Lewis

Requests for information should be addressed to:

Zonderkidz™
The children's group of Zondervan

Grand Rapids, Michigan 49530
www.zonderkidz.com

ISBN: 0-310-70299-2

Photography © by Wally McNamee/AFP/CORBIS
Additional Photography © by Reuters/Timepix
Cover Design: Lookout Design Group
Interior design by Todd Sprague
Printed in the United States of America

05 06 07 / DC/ 10 9 8 7 6 5 4

CONTENTS

1

FRIEND AND MENTOR

On February 2, 2001, a high school senior stood in the State Department of the United States and introduced Secretary of State Colin L. Powell.

He began by saying, "Hello, my name is Johnny Stone. I go to Ballou Senior High School. I'm a senior and my school is in D.C. I am Secretary Powell's e-mentee. We exchange e-mails on a regular basis, addressing my schoolwork and life in general. It has been a pleasure this past year to be able to get to know Secretary Powell through e-mail exchanges—he's a nice guy. And cool too. Now I would like to introduce my friend, my mentor, the secretary of state, Colin Powell."

Secretary Powell looked around the room. The students before him were attending Groundhog Job

Shadow Day, learning about the jobs of the adults in the State Department. It was an exciting day for them—a day made even more special by the opportunity to meet the first African-American secretary of state.

Secretary Powell thanked Johnny for introducing him and explained to the audience that the two of them had been getting to know each other by e-mail for the past six months. They had become good friends even though this was the first time they'd been able to meet face to face. "Hopefully, this is the beginning of a long relationship."

After welcoming everyone, Secretary Powell told the group that every year he looks forward to Groundhog Job Shadow Day. He deeply believes in this program, which allows young people from communities all across America to come into the workplace and see what adults—including "old" people like himself—do for a living and how they perform their jobs each day.

He went on to say, "You need to see what successful people are doing so that you can put yourself on that path to success. . . . At the end of the day, each and every one of you has to make a choice. Look in a mirror. Look at yourself. Look deep in your own heart and make a choice—a choice that says, 'I'm going to be a success. I don't care what obstacles are thrown in my way. I don't care what people say about me. . . . I'm going to be a success. I'm going to be a success because I *can* be a success.'"

Secretary of State Powell reminded the young people that God has given them strong bodies, healthy minds, and the ability to make good choices for their lives, if they are willing to use the tools God and their parents have given them. He told them, "Character is all about making those correct choices in life."

A few weeks later, Secretary of State Powell spotted a group of young people standing near the front door as he escorted the Dutch foreign minister out of the State Department after a formal lunch meeting.

"Hi! How are you, kids?" Colin Powell greeted them. Their nametags indicated they had come from all over the United States to visit the nation's capitol for the week as part of a youth program sponsored by the Senate. Secretary of State Powell introduced the children to the Dutch foreign minister, who seemed surprised to suddenly be surrounded by a group of boys and girls.

The group was lined up waiting to come through security, so Secretary Powell asked, "Where are you going?" The kids told him they had come to hear a speech about the State Department but didn't know who was to give the speech.

Smiling, Secretary Powell surprised the youngsters by saying, "Forget the speech. I have a better idea." Then he led the group upstairs to show them where he and other State Department officials meet and entertain foreign dignitaries at luncheons, receptions, and dinners. He escorted them through special diplomatic rooms furnished with beautiful antiques. In one room, he pointed out Thomas Jefferson's desk, on which, it is believed, Jefferson signed the Treaty of Paris, establishing American independence from Great Britain. Before the tour ended, forty kids and one slightly bewildered Dutch foreign minister received an unforgettable personal lesson in American history.

Why would a member of the president's cabinet take time to talk to a group of students and show them around the State Department? Why would a man who regularly meets with the world's top leaders take time to exchange regular e-mails with a high school kid?

Colin Powell does such things because he genuinely loves his country and its history. And he believes that if America is going to continue to be a great and influential nation, its people and especially its young people, need to understand their country's government and how it works. But there is another reason—although Colin Powell is now widely known and respected and has become one of the most influential leaders in the world, he has never forgotten who he is or how he came to be where he is today.

2

A CLOSE-KNIT FAMILY

Colin Powell was four years old when World War II began. And some of his earliest memories are of that war. He put together model airplane kits made of balsa wood, arranged play soldiers on the living room rug, and played out miniature make-believe battles. He and his friends staged bigger battles along the streets of their neighborhood, aiming imaginary guns at imaginary enemies.

"Bang, bang! You're dead!" one would say.

"I am not!" the other would answer.

And they would search the skies, looking for Nazi aircraft, just in case the enemy planes made it to New York City.

Everyone talked about the war because everyone knew someone fighting somewhere overseas.

One of Colin's most treasured possessions was a yellow Nazi Afrika Korps helmet, brought home from the war by his Uncle Vic, who served in the 4th Armored Division.

American military men and women were heroes in those days. Not just for young boys like Colin, but for Americans of all ages. People believed there was no greater honor than to bravely serve their country. And later in his life, that conviction no doubt influenced young Colin's attitude toward military service.

But World War II also had an immediate and personal impact on Colin Powell. It changed the way people said his name. Before the war he was "Cah-lin," the English pronunciation. But two days after the Japanese attack on Pearl Harbor, an Air Corps flier named Colin P. Kelly (pronounced "Coh-lin") became famous for attacking a Japanese battleship. So the boys in the neighborhood began calling Colin, Coh-lin, and it soon caught on with his friends and neighbors—though he would always be Cah-lin to his family.

That family included his father Luther Theophilus Powell, his mother Maud Ariel McKoy Powell—called Arie—and his older sister Marilyn. Luther and Arie had been born on the island of Jamaica. But they met only after they had each moved to New York City.

Luther was the second of nine children in a poor family. He had come to the United States as a young man, looking for a better life.

Arie was the oldest of nine children. Her mother, Alice McKoy—Colin's "Gram McKoy"—had immigrated to Havana, Cuba, then sent for Arie. At home in Jamaica, Arie had finished high school and was working as a stenographer in a lawyer's office. She agreed to join her mother, but only if they both moved to New York City.

When Luther arrived in the United States, he worked first as a gardener and then as a building superintendent. Finally he got a job at Ginsburgs, a women's clothing manufacturer. There he began in the stockroom, moved up to shipping clerk, and became a foreman in the shipping department.

Arie joined her mother in Cuba, and together they sailed to New York, where they found work as seamstresses in the garment district. Each week they would snip a ticket from each garment they had sewn, take their tickets in to work, and get paid according to the number of pieces of clothing they had completed. That type of sewing is called piecework.

In addition to doing piecework, Gram McKoy took in relatives and other immigrants from Jamaica as boarders. She sent most of the extra money she earned back to Jamaica to help other members of her family. According to Colin's Aunt Beryl, Luther

Powell met Arie McKoy when he rented a room from Gram McKoy.

Luther and Arie were married on December 28, 1929. Their daughter Marilyn was born in 1931 and their son Colin on April 5, 1937. The Powells were a hardworking couple. Luther would leave for work early in the morning and didn't return until seven or eight at night. Arie too would come home tired from working all day. Her goal was to earn enough money to give her children more chances in life than she had been given.

With great pride, Colin's parents became naturalized citizens of their new country, where they believed hard work and education would enable them (or at least their children) to achieve the American dream. But they never forgot their Jamaican roots—often feasting on traditional island fare such as plantains, roast goat, and rice and peas. And whenever anyone in the extended family talked about going home for a visit, it was understood they meant returning to Jamaica.

Although they never had a lot of money, the Powells were respected in their neighborhood. Luther was known to be a friendly and outgoing neighbor, always willing to help those in need. When the gas man came by to read the meter, Luther always invited him in to sit at the kitchen table and share a cup of coffee. At Christmas time, Luther would bring the garbage men into the apartment so he could offer them some refreshments and present them with their annual holiday tip.

Luther Powell was the kind of person people said "never met a stranger." His family remembers times when he'd sit out on the front stoop of their apartment building, waiting for someone to come along. He would then engage that person in conversation and invite him or her in for coffee or tea. That open, welcoming nature is one of the traits he passed along to his son.

One of Colin's earliest memories—a traumatic one—involved another family member. One day when he was four years old, his Gram McKoy was watching him while his parents worked. Colin found a hairpin and stuck it into an electrical outlet. He saw a blinding flash of light and felt the electrical shock. His Gram scolded him and hugged him at the same time. When his parents came home, they reprimanded him again. But, even at that early age, all the fussing made Colin feel loved and cared for.

When Colin was six years old, his family moved from Harlem, where he had been born. They settled in a tenement building on Kelly Street in the South Bronx, another borough in New York City, where they occupied a four-bedroom apartment on the third floor. Each floor of the four-story tenement building had two apartments. So seven other families lived in that building. It was there that Colin remembers growing up.

When Colin stood in front of the building where he lived, he was only three blocks from his elementary school. And just beyond the school was St. Margaret's Episcopal Church, where the Powells had their family pew. His Aunt Gytha and Uncle Alfred lived across the street. Aunt Laurice and Uncle Vic's place was down the street. And Colin's godmother, Aunt Vads, lived just a little farther down.

Hunts Point Park was also a short distance from their apartment. Shortly after they moved to the Bronx, Colin went with his mother and Marilyn to the park to play. Arie pushed Marilyn on the swing while Colin watched and waited for his turn. Finally Colin thought he had waited long enough: It was time for his turn on the swing. When Marilyn didn't agree, Colin ran in front of her. The swing hit Colin on the head. The resulting cut required stitches and left a permanent scar.

In later years, the Hunts Point section of New York became a violent, crime-ridden part of the city. For a time, drug pushers and gangs ran so wild that the local police precinct was nicknamed Fort Apache. But during the years that Colin Powell was growing up, Hunts Point was a small neighborhood, where everyone knew everyone else. And if a kid misbehaved, some adult, often a relative, usually saw it and came out to reprimand him.

Still, the neighborhood was rough enough that the Powells kept their doors and windows locked.

And at night, they propped a steel rod against the front door, so no one could push the door in. Colin knew about burglaries and street fights that happened nearby. But he felt surrounded by people who loved him and were watching out for him.

Kelly Street, a block away from the Powells' home, was curved, and everyone called the surrounding area Banana Kelly.

Like almost every block in the Bronx, there was a candy store here, usually run by European Jews, who sold school supplies, candy, ice cream, and soft drinks. Every few blocks, there would be a Jewish bakery, a Puerto Rican grocery store, a Chinese laundry, and an Italian shoe repair shop. But Colin did not know of any business owned by a black person.

Banana Kelly had no majority, so everyone was a minority: either a Jew, or a Pole, or a Greek, or an Italian, or a Puerto Rican, or a Negro (as African-Americans were called in those days).

Colin's best childhood friend was Gene Norman, who was also West Indian. Another close friend, Tony Grant, was white. Other friends had names such as Ramirez, Schwartz, and Garcia.

Colin remembers that all the various ethnic minorities of his neighborhood boiled down to just two groups: the ones who used drugs and the ones who didn't. He and his friends didn't use drugs.

In later years, Colin would talk to young people about drugs. In a speech on April 15, 1991, at Morris High School, he told the students that there were lots of drugs in the neighborhood where he grew up. But he never touched them—not even to experiment.

"One, my parents would have killed me," he said, "but the second reason is . . . it was stupid."

He and his friends knew it was a terribly destructive way to treat the life God and their parents had given them.

3

SURROUNDED BY LOVE

When Colin was eight years old, his family, along with some aunts and uncles, took a summer vacation on Long Island. Colin was outside by himself playing, when a piece of dirt flew into his eye. He ran into the cabin, crying. His Aunt Laurice got the dirt out of his eye. But the eye still hurt and Colin continued crying. When he finally stopped and went back outside to play, he overheard his aunt.

"That boy is such a crybaby!" she told his Aunt Gytha.

That hurt Colin's feelings. And he thought, *I'm never going to let anyone see me cry again!* But it was a vow he wasn't able to keep.

The following year, Colin went into fourth grade at P.S. (Public School) 39, where he was put into the bottom class, called Four Up. Colin knew that meant the teachers thought he was a little slow. He felt embarrassed and knew it would worry his parents.

For the Powell and McKoy families, education was the way to get up and out of poverty. Marilyn, Colin's sister, was an honor student and expected to go to college. Colin knew his parents thought it was important to excel in school, and he wasn't measuring up to their hopes for him.

Colin took piano lessons for a while. But that was not a success either. Then he tried playing the flute. Marilyn laughed at the sounds that came out of Colin's instrument. After a short time, he dropped those lessons as well.

To make matters worse, Colin wasn't much of an athlete. One day Colin and some friends were playing baseball in a vacant lot when Colin's father walked by and stopped to watch the game.

Colin came up to bat. He swung at the first pitch—and missed. Next pitch—strike two. He tried to forget that his father was watching. The pitcher threw the ball again, and Colin took another big swing—strike three. He was out. Colin struck out every time he came up to bat that day. He was embarrassed to do so poorly in front of his father, even though Luther Powell never expressed any disappointment.

But Colin didn't need to be the best athlete to be happy with his life. He enjoyed playing a variety of other neighborhood games, such as stickball, stoopball, punchball, sluggo, hot beans and butter, tossing marbles, and shooting checkers. His friend Tony once added up the games they played in the neighborhood and came up with a total of thirty-six.

One of Colin's favorites was kite-fighting. He and his friends would smash up glass bottles, then lay a can containing the pieces of glass on the trolley tracks until the cars had crushed the glass into powder. They glued the powdered glass onto their kite strings. They also fastened double-edged razor blades to their kite's tail. Then they flew the kites from the roofs of the apartment buildings, diving and dodging the kite so that the string or the razor blades would cut down the kites of boys on other rooftops. They cheered as their opponent's kite fluttered to the street. It was their version of a World War II air battle.

Colin was also well known for a game called ring-a-levio, a Bronx version of capture the flag. Each side would choose four, maybe six, boys. Then one group would run and the other would chase. When someone got caught, they were put in a den, any enclosed area nearby. The prisoners could be freed by having someone on their side get inside the den and yell, "Free all!" Some of the boys would try to sneak into the enclosure. But Colin preferred a blitz. He would watch for the moment when he thought his opponents had edged far enough away.

Then he'd run full speed from half a block away into the den to free all his captured teammates.

Another thing Colin did really well, and enjoyed doing, was his job as acolyte at St. Margaret's Episcopal Church. Luther was senior warden, a lay leader, at St. Margaret's. Arie was the head of the altar guild, and Marilyn played the piano at the children's service. The Powell family helped out with the church bazaar, bake sale, and annual dance, and Sundays found the Powells seated in their family pew.

Luther and Arie had been raised in the Anglican Church in Jamaica. St. Margaret's, with its formal style of worship, spires, altars, and priests, reminded them of those churches. And Colin loved the majesty, pomp, and ritual of the formal, high-church services. He enjoyed the smell of incense and the sight of candles lit in worship.

His confirmation was a memorable and meaningful experience for him. A bishop placed his hands on Colin's head as the boy knelt at the altar. Then the bishop prayed: "Defend, O Lord, this Thy child with Thy heavenly grace; that he may continue to be Thine forever; and daily increase in Thy Holy Spirit more and more, until he comes unto thy everlasting kingdom. Amen."

Colin later said that his confirmation experience gave him a deep sense of assurance. "After that, every time I heard those words, I knew that God was watching over me. And I knew that I needed to live up to his expectations."

Marilyn's first boyfriend was a young man named John, whose family also attended St. Margaret's church. And Colin was a typical, annoying little brother. He would sneak up on Marilyn and John when they were alone and bother them. Sometimes John would give Colin a quarter, just to get him to leave them alone.

Marilyn returned the favor, several years later, when Colin brought his high school girlfriend to a family party. Marilyn giggled at them most of the evening. Later, when Colin asked her what she had found so funny, Marilyn answered with a question, "What is so special about that girl?" Colin was surprised to realize that his sister didn't think his girl was special. And Marilyn's opinion mattered to him. He broke up with that girlfriend not long after.

When Colin went to elementary school at P.S. 39, he would walk out of his building, turn right, and walk just three blocks. His junior high school, P.S. 52—an all-boys school—was only one more block past that. When it was time to go to high school, all Colin had to do was walk outside, turn left instead of right, and walk a few blocks in that direction.

Marilyn had attended prestigious Walton High School and was an honor student there. Colin applied to attend Stuyvesant High School, another selective school. But his school guidance counselor wrote, "We advise against it" on his report card, and he was unable to get in. Colin Powell still has that report card.

So Colin went to Morris High School in the South Bronx. Unlike his sister, he had not yet found anything that he was really good at and liked to do. He was just an average boy, making average grades in school and having a good time in life.

Colin may not have been a talented musician, but he enjoyed listening to the calypso music played at the frequent family get-togethers. He may not have been an outstanding athlete, but he liked playing neighborhood games. And he may not have been an honor student, but he was a happy boy surrounded by the love and care of his family.

He knew his parents worked hard to provide for him and his sister. He also knew they expected him to "make something of himself." So more than anything else he wanted to please them— make them proud. So he determined to do that, even if he didn't yet know how.

4

ACCEPTING RESPONSIBILITY

One summer, during his high school years, Colin was selected to go away to church camp. And at camp he made some new friends, boys who were not a good influence on Colin. He and his new buddies sneaked out of camp and bought some beer. They put the beer in a toilet tank to cool it and keep it hidden. They thought their secret was safe. Who would look there?

Someone did. The camp officials knew what they had found. But they did not know who had put it there.

The priest who served as camp director called everyone together. He did not yell at the campers or accuse anyone. He explained what had been discovered. Then he asked who was ready to accept responsibility for the misdeed. Who would own up like a man?

The priest's calm approach spoke to Colin's conscience. Colin stood up and said, "Father, I did it." Two of his accomplices heard Colin and also stood to confess. They could have stayed silent and gotten away with the mischief. But instead they chose to be honest.

The camp still sent them home and contacted their parents. All the way home on the train, Colin knew that he would have to face his parents with what he had done. He knew his behavior had embarrassed them. Being thrown out of church camp was worse than striking out in baseball. Worse than failing at piano or flute. Even worse than being in the slow class at school.

Colin slowly walked home, where his mother met him with a scowl on her face. And when she finished talking to him, it was his father's turn. Colin dreaded that. He hated the fact that he had done something to disappoint his dad.

But in the middle of Luther Powell's lecture, the phone rang. On the line was Father Weeden, the priest at St. Margaret's—the man who had chosen Colin to go to camp. He wanted Luther and Arie Powell to know the whole story. What Colin had done was wrong. But, he told them, "Your Colin stood up and took responsibility."

That one phone call changed the family's disgrace to pride. And Colin learned a powerful lesson about honesty and the importance of accepting responsibility for his actions.

One afternoon, when Colin was fourteen years old, he walked to the post office to mail some letters for his mother. On the way he passed Sickser's, a baby furniture store. Mr. Sickser, the owner, stopped him and asked if he wanted to earn some money. That sounded good to Colin, so he followed the older man around to a warehouse behind the store and agreed to unload a truck full of Christmas merchandise for the store.

By the time Mr. Sickser came back to check, Colin was almost done with the job.

"So, you're a worker!" Mr. Sickser exclaimed. He offered Colin a job working after school and on Saturdays. Colin continued to work at Sickser's throughout high school and his first years of college. He unloaded trucks, assembled cribs and baby carriages, and every December, put toys together and set up the holiday displays. For this work, Colin earned between fifty cents and seventy-five cents an hour.

Mr. Sickser and many of his customers were Jewish and spoke Yiddish. While working there, Colin learned to speak and understand some of that language, which served him and his employer well.

Sometimes Mr. Sickser would ask Colin to escort some of his customers up to see the better merchandise on the second floor. They would examine the strollers and furniture, and then, figuring this black youngster wouldn't know what they were saying, they'd use Yiddish to talk about which item they liked best and what was the most they would pay. Colin would report what he'd overheard to Mr. Sickser, who would then climb the stairs and use the information to close the sale.

Another way Colin earned money was by turning the lights on and off at an Orthodox Jewish synagogue near his home. Each Friday he earned a quarter performing this task so that the worshipers could observe the ban on Sabbath work.

Colin tried out for and made the track team in high school. He even did well enough to get a letter in track. But he found the training—running cross-country through Van Cortlandt Park—boring, and after one season, he dropped off the team.

Colin also played basketball for his church team. He was tall and fast, and the coach thought he would be a good player. But he and the coach soon found out that wasn't the case. He didn't like sitting on the bench, so Colin quit that too.

One thing Colin did like was hanging out with his friends. One of their favorite activities was making the walk down Kelly Street, up 163rd Street, around Southern Boulevard, up Westchester Avenue, and back home. On Saturday mornings he and his friends would go to the movie theater, where they would pay a quarter to watch a double feature.

All the boys in Banana Kelly looked forward to getting bikes in much the same way kids today anticipate buying a car. Colin's first bike was a Columbia racer with twenty-six-inch balloon tires, one of the nicest bikes a kid could have. That was typical of Luther Powell. He wanted his children to have the best of everything.

Colin rode that bicycle everywhere. He and his friend Gene Norman loved to race each other. The boys could get almost anywhere on their bikes. But for those trips where their bikes wouldn't do, they could take the subway or trolley.

Some weekends, Colin and Gene would take a trolley car to the George Washington Bridge. They'd walk across the bridge into New Jersey and camp overnight in the woods.

In 1952 Marilyn called home from college to tell her parents that she was in love with a young man named Norm Berns. The two wanted to get married, so Marilyn asked to bring him home to meet her family. She also told her parents that Norm was white. An interracial marriage concerned Luther Powell. He knew that such couples faced many difficulties. He liked Marilyn's boyfriend, and Norm was obviously very much in love with Marilyn. But Luther insisted that they wait at least a year, to think over their decision.

In the meantime, the Powells traveled to meet Norm's family in Buffalo, New York, four hundred miles from the South Bronx. What an adventure for Colin! He felt as if he were headed for the wild West! He had never before been so far from Hunts Point. The visit was a successful one. The Berns family seemed to love and admire Marilyn, and the Powells thought the Bernses were fine people.

In August 1953 Marilyn married Norm Berns. The wedding reception was held at the Concourse Plaza Hotel, the biggest hotel in the Bronx. This was Luther Powell's only daughter's wedding, and he wanted nothing but the best.

Marilyn graduated from Buffalo State Teachers College in 1952 and became a bilingual schoolteacher in Southern California. She and Norm have now been married almost fifty years. They have two daughters and one granddaughter.

In February 1954 Colin Powell graduated from Morris High School. As a result of an accelerated school program, he finished early, before his seventeenth birthday. His high school grade point average was 78.3—just below a C. He still wasn't the scholar his sister was, and he wasn't at all sure he was cut out for college.

5

A PLACE TO BELONG

Colin did go to college for one reason: Luther and Arie Powell expected him to. He applied to attend New York University and City College of New York, and he was accepted by both schools, in spite of his high school grades. Making the decision between the two was easy. New York University, a private college, cost $750 a year, and City College of New York (CCNY) cost $10 a year. Colin went to CCNY.

In February 1954, still only sixteen, Colin started college. On a bitter cold, blustery winter morning, he boarded a bus and rode to the campus of City College of New York. Once there, he looked around at the college buildings and felt overwhelmed.

"Hey, kid! You new?" a friendly voice boomed at him. Raymond the bagel man—called that although he sold pretzels—became Colin's first friend at college. Raymond was a fixture at CCNY, standing behind his large, steaming cart of warm, soft pretzels. And over the next four and a half years, Colin bought more pretzels than he could count, stopping to shoot the breeze with Raymond.

As Colin walked across campus to his first class, he passed the ROTC drill hall. Colin paid little attention. He had no way of knowing that building would eventually become the center of his college life.

Colin's first college major was engineering—not because he was good at math or science but because his mother felt it was the best option. Engineering, according to Arie Powell, who had talked with a number of relatives about her son's future, was "where the money was." Colin did well for one semester as an engineering major. The following summer, he took an introductory engineering course and decided to change his major to geology.

During his first term, Colin was intrigued by students who walked around campus in uniforms. In the fall of 1954 he asked about and then joined the Reserve Officers Training Corps (ROTC). He stood in line and was issued olive-drab pants and a jacket, a brown shirt, brown tie, brown shoes, a belt with a brass buckle, and an overseas cap.

Dressed in that uniform, Colin looked in the mirror and liked what he saw.

ROTC gave Colin a place to belong. For the first time in his life, he felt he was part of a brotherhood. The discipline, structure, and camaraderie were all things that Colin had longed for. And it made him feel distinctive—something he had never felt before.

He survived his other classes. He even enjoyed his geology classes. But he lived to go to ROTC. At last he had found the one thing he really wanted to do.

The ROTC had three military societies on campus: the Webb Patrol, Scabbard and Blade, and the Pershing Rifles. Colin joined the Pershing Rifles, because they were the elite of the three groups. Members of the Pershing Rifles wore blue-and-white shoulder cords and enamel crests on their uniforms. Colin discovered that he liked the uniforms and the symbols of the military.

One young black member of the Pershing Rifles caught Colin's eye. He was a cadet leader and an officer. His name was Ronnie Brooks, and he became Colin's mentor. Ronnie was a cadet sergeant, so Colin became a cadet sergeant. Colin followed in Ronnie's footsteps to be a battalion commander, a drillmaster, and a pledge officer.

Colin spent most Saturdays practicing with the Pershing Rifle drill team. He learned how to draw an M–1 rifle and perform the Queen Mary salute. He worked hard to master the rifle spins and special types of precision marching.

The Pershing Rifle drill teams competed against ROTC drill teams from other colleges and universities in the New York City area. The competitions had two categories: regular drill and trick drill. Ronnie Brooks led the Pershing Rifle regular drill team, and Colin was placed in charge of the trick drill team.

During Colin's junior year, Ronnie's team scored 460 points out of a possible 500 points in their competition. Then Colin took his eighteen-man team out on the floor. They had shined their shoes so well that they could see their faces reflected in the gleam.

Most drill team captains just marked time as the team did their maneuvers. So when Colin did a dance solo to a step called the camel walk, to mark his team's time, the crowd watching the competition cheered. His trick drill team scored 492 points out of the possible 500 points, and the Pershing Rifles took first place.

The following summer, just before his senior year of college, Colin went to Fort Bragg, North Carolina, for ROTC summer training. There, he and his Pershing Rifle friends learned how to set up roadblocks, practiced on the rifle range, and learned how to fire 81mm mortars. His superiors at Fort Bragg had heard about his honors as a drill team captain and named him the acting company commander.

At the end of six weeks, the cadets were judged on course grades, rifle range scores, physical fitness, and leadership. Colin was given a desk set with two pens set in holders on a marble base. On the base was engraved "Best Cadet, Company D." Another student was the "Best Cadet" for the encampment. Colin came in second for that honor.

Colin was thrilled about his achievement until a sergeant told him something that disturbed him. "You want to know why you didn't get best cadet in the camp?" asked the sergeant. "These Southern ROTC instructors are not going to say that the best kid here was a Negro."

Colin didn't want to believe the officer's statement was true. But he drove home from North Carolina with two white officers from CCNY. Everywhere they stopped on that long drive home had three restrooms: Men, Women, and Colored. While his friends could use the men's room, Colin had to use the colored restroom. He didn't feel safe again until they were north of Baltimore, Maryland.

But he brought his trophy home to show his parents—the desk set with the words "Best Cadet, Company D." Here was proof that he had excelled in his chosen field. And he had proven to himself that he was good at one thing: He was a good leader.

Years later, Colin Powell carefully placed that desk set on his desk in his office at the Pentagon. Even as chairman of the Joint Chiefs of Staff, he continued to be proud of that early achievement.

When Colin started college, he still worked for Sickser's baby furniture store. But by the next summer he decided that he needed a job with better pay, so he found a job at a furniture plant, screwing hinges on cabinets. Then he got a job as a porter in a Pepsi-Cola bottling plant. He wasn't sure what a porter did until he arrived for his first day of work and someone handed him a mop.

If earning $65 per week meant he had to mop, Colin would mop. He soon learned that mopping front to back is hard on the back, so he learned to mop from side to side. And Colin decided if he was going to mop, he would do a good job. He would mop until the floor shined. It was hard work — especially the day someone dropped fifty cases of Pepsi-Cola from a forklift and Colin was called to mop up the mess.

Colin noticed that all the porters mopping floors were black. All the workers on the bottling machines were white. And the white employees earned more money.

At the end of the summer, a foreman came to Colin and said, "Kid, you mop pretty good."

"You gave me plenty of opportunity to learn," Colin answered.

The foreman told him that he could have a job the next summer, and Colin answered, "Not behind a mop." So the following summer, Colin got a job on the bottling machine and soon became the deputy shift leader.

He had learned a valuable lesson: Always do your best. Someone may be watching.

While Colin was in college, his neighborhood was changing. And each time Colin went home, he could see that things were getting worse. Gang fights had become gang wars. The kids who had used marijuana were now using heroin. Once he came home and found that a person he knew had died of a drug overdose.

Now at family get-togethers, his relatives talked about when they could move away from Hunts Point. One by one, members of his family "got out." Aunt Laurice and Colin's godmother, Aunt Vads, moved to the northern, upper part of the Bronx. His Aunt Dot moved to Queens, another borough of New York City. And Sunday after Sunday, after they went to church, Luther and Arie Powell looked at houses in the upper Bronx and Queens.

In 1956 the Powells bought a house in Queens, in a neighborhood in transition. The white families were moving out, and black families were moving in. They bought from one of the last white families moving out.

Now Colin commuted to school by subway from Queens instead of from Hunts Point.

Colin's junior year in college, Anthony "Tony" Mavroudis joined the Pershing Rifles and became one of Colin's closest college friends. Tony was Greek-American. He also commuted from Queens and worked part-time as an auto mechanic. He and

Colin became as close as brothers. They commuted, dated, trained, studied, and did everything together.

His senior year of college, Colin was named cadet colonel over the CCNY regiment of one thousand cadets. And he was company commander of the Pershing Rifles.

By the end of his last year of college, Colin became a Distinguished Military Graduate. For this reason, he was offered a regular commission rather than a reserve commission—he would serve in the military for three years, rather than two.

On June 9, 1958, wearing a new uniform his father had paid for, Colin was commissioned as an officer in the U.S. Army. Luther and Arie Powell looked on as Colin repeated the oath with his fellow classmates:

"I, Colin Powell, do solemnly swear that I will support and defend the Constitution of the United States against all enemies, foreign and domestic, and that I will well and faithfully discharge the duties of the office upon which I am about to enter, so help me God."

One day later, in a ceremony that seemed less important to Colin, but of more importance to his mother, Colin graduated from college. He'd completed another major milestone in his life. And this time, he knew what he was going to do next.

6

BASIC TRAINING

While Colin was in college, the world around him had been changing.

In 1954, during his first year at CCNY, three important events took place—events that would have a significant impact on America. First, the U.S. detonated a hydrogen bomb six hundred times more powerful than the one dropped at Hiroshima. Second, the French army lost a battle to the Communists in the small, little-known country of Vietnam. And third, in a case called *Brown v. Board of Education*, the U.S. Supreme Court ordered an end to the segregation of black children from white children in public schools.

Less than a year later, during Colin's second year of college, the conflict in Vietnam began to escalate. A quarter-million people fled from North Vietnam into South Vietnam, bringing the total number of refugees there to half a million.

The following year, 1956, an African-American woman named Rosa Parks was arrested for refusing to sit in the back of a bus in Montgomery, Alabama. And a young preacher named Dr. Martin Luther King Jr. was jailed for his nonviolent protests. In the fall of 1957, as Colin was returning to school, troops escorted nine black students into Central High School in Little Rock, Arkansas.

Things were going well for Colin. He had now decided what he wanted to do with his life, and he won honors in ROTC, the part of his college career that he cared about most. The conflicts going on in the world might as well have been happening on another planet. But they would soon intrude upon Colin's life.

When Colin finished college and boarded on a Greyhound bus headed for Fort Benning, Georgia, Luther Powell was concerned. His son was headed for infantry training in the South, where people were demonstrating and society seemed out of control. He felt it was a dangerous place to send his only son.

Even Colin's ROTC commanding officer, Colonel Brookhart, took Colin aside and cautioned him to be careful. He told Colin that the South was a different world from the one he had been used to.

He would be required to compromise, accept things he could not change, and, above all, learn not to rock the boat.

The concept of racism was relatively new to Colin. And his world was just beginning to unfold in front of him. Focusing on one goal, he headed for Georgia, determined to become the best soldier he could be.

Colin began his official military career on a sunny day in June 1958. He was a newly commissioned lieutenant when he mustered in front of the infantry school at Fort Benning on his first day of basic training. A statue of a bronze infantryman stood there, with a rifle held high, leading men into battle.

Basic training included classroom work and weapons training—even more challenging was the field training. Colin had to hike for five miles, at night, with only a compass to guide him to a stake in the ground somewhere in the middle of nowhere.

By the end of basic training, Colin and his fellow officers had learned that their job was to go into battle first—like the soldier depicted in that bronze statue—demonstrating courage, determination, and sacrifice. In later years, Colin would tell younger officers that he learned most of what he knew about military life in those first eight weeks of basic training.

Colin finished basic training in the top ten of his class. Then he signed on for two months of Ranger school. This included an exercise called Slide for Life. The Ranger trainees would climb a tree to reach a pulley. The pulley ran along a cable that had been attached to two trees on opposite sides of a river. The students would grab a hook attached to the pulley, an instructor would give them a push, and they would slide, very fast, from one side to the other.

The challenge was to hang on to the rope until the instructor yelled, "Drop!" This was far from easy as they watched the second tree come rushing toward them.

Colin spent a couple of weeks in a Florida swamp, eating alligator and rattlesnakes. Then they moved to north Georgia and learned to scale cliffs and patrol in the dark in waist-deep water. Colin and the other students slept on the ground. They mastered the Australian rappel, which required them to move down the face of a cliff on a rope—face first!

When Ranger school ended, Colin went to airborne training. The first week, he dropped just a few feet to the ground. The second week, he jumped from a 250-foot training tower, using a parachute. By the third week, he was ready for the real thing. Colin and his fellow trainees took off in a transport plane. When the plane reached the right height, Colin stood in the open door of the plane, felt the wind in his face, and jumped—the first of five jumps in two days.

On the base, in the swamp, in camp, Colin knew that he was one of the best. But every time he left the post, he was confronted by the racism his father had warned him about. Off the base he was treated as a second-class citizen. He could go into stores and buy things, but he couldn't eat at a restaurant or go to a men's room.

And attending church was a problem. The nearest black congregation was a Baptist church, quite a distance from the post. The army provided Colin with a truck and a driver to take him there. But after a few weeks, the driver, a white corporal, talked to Colin. He was glad to drive Colin to church, he said, but that meant he missed his own services. Would it be possible for him to join Colin in the black church?

Colin thought that would be fine, but the black Baptist minister thought otherwise. He was afraid that a white serviceman attending a black church would get into trouble with the local white people. So the corporal waited in the truck.

The injustices of racism weighed heavily on Colin. He knew his first priority was to do his best in the army. Allowing himself to be provoked into a rage could damage his military career. But he also knew that he was not inferior to anyone, and he refused to let anyone make him feel that way. He made up his mind that nothing he encountered off the base would keep him from doing his best on the base. He would show them!

After he finished basic training, Ranger school, and airborne training, Colin returned home on leave to see his family and spend time with his girlfriend. Afterwards, he received military orders to report to the 3rd Armored Division in West Germany. Gelnhausen was only forty-three miles from Soviet-occupied territory.

The cold war between the United States and the Soviet Union was in full swing. Colin and the other American soldiers assigned to guard the Fulda Gap assumed that the Russians might attack any day. Colin was an officer, a platoon leader in charge of forty men, and whatever happened, Colin's job was to hold his position and take care of those men, some of them his age and some older.

Several times during his tour in Germany, Colin was pulled off his regular assignment for unusual duties. Once he was given the task of prosecuting three army truck drivers who were on trial for killing three German civilians. The truck drivers had been racing five-ton army trucks along a German road when one of the trucks skidded out of control and hit a car.

The soldiers hired professional lawyers to defend them. Colin was just a young infantry lieutenant, but he read everything he could about the case and the laws related to it, and he argued persuasively. He won convictions against two of the defendants.

Colin successfully fulfilled other responsibilities while in Germany. He was given the command of a division pistol team and led them to the championship. Once, he was an assistant adjutant at brigade headquarters. And for two months, he commanded an honor guard.

On July 20, 1959, a superior officer wrote a report concerning Lieutenant Powell. It stated that Colin was "tenacious, firm, yet polished in manner and can deal with individuals of any rank. His potential for a career in the military is unlimited...." Colin was only twenty-two years old at the time.

Colin did make a few mistakes, however. One day his new company commander overheard him shouting at another lieutenant over the phone. In his next report, the officer cited Colin's "quick temper." That was the only negative comment Colin had received since he first put on a uniform in ROTC at CCNY.

His company commander explained to him that when you lose your temper, you often also lose the respect of those who see you out of control. That report—and the commander's words—helped Colin learn how important it is to keep your emotions under control.

Early one morning during his duty in Germany, Colin saw a little of what real war was like. He was returning to his brigade with some rations for the mess hall, when he heard an odd, whistling sound over his head. He stopped and watched as an eight-inch artillery shell hit a tent pole and detonated. Colin dropped the food he had been carrying and pushed his way through smoke and fumes to the tent that had been hit. A dozen soldiers had been killed while they slept, and more were wounded. They had been paid the day before, and Colin saw pieces of money mixed in with the debris. The shell had been fired by American soldiers who were target practicing. The officers who had misaligned that gun were relieved of duty.

By December 1960, Colin had finished his two-year tour in Germany. He was now the commanding officer of Delta Company, though he was only a lieutenant and commanding officers were usually at least captains. Colin was asked to stay in Germany, but he turned down the assignment, choosing instead to spend some time at home with his family and his girlfriend.

The army assigned Colin to Fort Devens, Massachusetts, thirty miles from Boston and just a few hours' drive from New York City. His first assignment was as a liaison officer. Then he became executive officer of Company A. That meant he was second in command. After a short time, however, the company commander was reassigned, and Colin was once again placed in command of a company, though he was still only a first lieutenant.

While he was company commander, Colin invented a number of competitions for his troops—

best barracks, best day room, best weapons inspection. He remembered how much the drill team competitions had meant to him during ROTC. And he knew that the more competitions the soldiers participated in, the more opportunities each one would have to be a winner. He wanted all his troops to feel like winners.

When Colin left Company A, he became adjutant of a new unit, the 1st Battalion, 2nd Infantry. His new job was to handle personnel, promotions, assignments, discipline, mail, and "morale and welfare."

As part of that job, Colin's commanding officer instructed him to send out "Welcome Baby" letters to all the men in their battalion whose wives had babies. Each baby's birth meant two letters—one to the mother congratulating the parents and another to the baby, welcoming the child into the battalion. And Colin was expected to send the letters on the day the baby was born.

Colin was not excited about such a mundane assignment and sometimes did not take care of it promptly, which earned him a reprimand from his commanding officer. As he began to take the task more seriously, he realized the mothers of the babies and the fathers (his soldiers) greatly appreciated the letters. The letters helped the fathers feel important and cared for in what could often be an impersonal army. The mothers wrote back, thanking the battalion for including them in their husband's army life.

Colin learned how important such small touches could be. And that experience helped him begin to learn another lesson that served him well later in his career—the army is more than just a thing, an organization, or even a system. It's made up of men and women who appreciate being treated as individuals.

Colin was still at Fort Devens in the summer of 1961. He had served his three years and could leave the army at any time. That is what his family expected him to do. They were surprised when Colin told them he had decided to stay in the army. But that was not all he wanted to do.

7

STARTING A FAMILY

While he had been stationed in Germany in the summer of 1959, Colin had come home on leave. During his visit, he and his girlfriend had discussed marriage. Late one night, Colin turned to his father for advice: Should they get married right away?

Luther's response had been quick and definite. "You're not ready for marriage," he told Colin. Knowing that he would not see his girlfriend again for another sixteen months, Colin returned to Germany. By the time he was reassigned to the U.S., the relationship was over, and he realized his father had been right.

One day in November 1961, Colin was in the bachelor officer's quarters (BOQ) at Fort Devens. A friend walked in and asked him for a favor. His girlfriend lived in Boston, so would Colin come to Boston with him and go out with his girlfriend's roommate? Colin had never before been on a blind date, and he wasn't sure it was a good idea. But he agreed to go.

The girl he met that night was Alma Johnson. Alma had not been interested in going on a blind date either. In fact, she was angry with her roommate for talking her into it. So Alma decided to dress weird and put on a lot of makeup to discourage any interest her date might have in her. However, after seeing Colin, she had a sudden change of mind. She slipped back into her room, changed clothes, and cleaned off the extra makeup.

Colin had such a good time that he called Alma the next day and asked for another date. Soon the two were seeing each other regularly.

Alma had grown up in Birmingham, Alabama, the daughter of a high school principal. After high school, she attended Fisk University in Nashville, Tennessee. After receiving her degree, she had been a radio hostess on her own program, "Luncheon with Alma." She gave the listeners household hints and played music. Alma had moved to Boston to attend graduate school. When Colin met her she was an audiologist, driving a van throughout the area, giving hearing tests.

During the Christmas holidays, Colin took Alma to meet his family. At a New Year's Eve party in the basement of Luther's and Arie's home,

Alma was introduced to aunts, uncles, and cousins and to the dancing, laughing, eating, and singing chaos of a Jamaican party. Colin's family liked Alma and approved of the match. This was a good thing, because Colin was in love.

In August 1962, after serving at Fort Devens for eighteen months, Colin received orders to go to South Vietnam as a military advisor. He was to report to Fort Bragg, North Carolina, for a five-week course, after which he would be promoted to captain before leaving for his new duty station.

Colin called his parents with the good news. Then he called Alma. She didn't seem excited, so he drove to Boston to explain to her why this was such a good opportunity. Only the best and brightest officers were being sent to Vietnam as advisors. Colin had always considered himself one of the best with a bright future in the military. This assignment was evidence that his superior officers felt the same way.

Alma wanted to know what this would mean for their relationship. So Colin told her: The assignment would be for one year, and he hoped that she would write him often.

"I'm not going to write," she answered. "If I'm nothing more than a pen pal to you, we might as well end it now."

Colin went back to Fort Devens to think. He loved Alma. His parents loved her. She was beautiful, intelligent, and a good friend. Why was he waiting? Colin didn't know.

The next morning, he drove back to Boston and asked Alma Johnson to marry him. She said yes, and they decided to get married in two weeks.

At first Luther Powell didn't want to attend his son's wedding in Birmingham. He was still nervous about visiting the South, where he felt he would be treated as a second-class citizen. But when Marilyn and Norman, Colin's sister and her husband, decided to go, Luther changed his mind. They had a wedding and reception in Birmingham, then another reception in New York not long afterward.

One month after the wedding, Colin said farewell to Fort Devens and headed to training in Fort Bragg. Driving through the South with his new wife was unnerving. While on that trip, they had trouble finding restrooms available to blacks. They had to stop by the side of the road.

Even worse, when they began looking for a house to live in near Fort Bragg, the only places available to a black couple were dilapidated and overgrown with weeds. The real estate agent offered to let them stay in his home, but his house was little better than the shabby places they had already turned down.

Sad and discouraged, Colin and Alma decided that Alma would have to live with her parents in Birmingham, while Colin stayed at Fort Bragg. They were heartbroken to face this separation, in addition to being apart for the year Colin expected to be in Vietnam. And they already knew that Alma was pregnant with their first child.

But, on what looked to be their last evening together for a long time, Colin and Alma had dinner with Joe and Pat Schwar. Joe, a white officer, had been a friend of Colin in Germany. He and Pat had three small sons and lived in a three-bedroom military duplex on the post at Fort Bragg. When they learned of the Powells' dilemma, the Schwars insisted that Colin and Alma move in with them. So, for the five weeks that Colin was in training at Fort Bragg, he and Alma lived in the Schwars' boys' bedroom, while the boys slept in the room with their baby brother. The Powells were grateful. A few people acted surprised that a white family would take in a black couple, but the Schwars and the Powells developed a friendship that was to last a lifetime.

Colin's five weeks of training included studying French colonial history—since Vietnam had been a French colony. And he learned to speak a little of the Vietnamese language.

When his training ended shortly before Christmas, Colin and Alma said good-bye to the Schwars and headed for Birmingham. That's where Alma planned to stay while Colin was overseas. Her parents and her aunt and uncle had built a house outside of the city for the four of them. They had a spare room for Alma and the baby she was carrying. Colin was relieved that Alma's father would be there to watch over her while he was gone.

Since Colin's orders were to leave by December 23, the family celebrated Christmas early that year. They found a Christmas tree, decorated it, and exchanged gifts. Alma's mother gave the couple matching tape recorders so that they could make audiotapes to send each other while they were apart.

Two days before Christmas, Colin said goodbye to his pregnant wife and went to the airport by himself. He arrived in Saigon, South Vietnam, on Christmas Day 1962.

8

FACING DISCRIMINATION

Eight years before Colin and Alma married, the people of a small southeast Asian nation called French Indochina had overthrown the colonial government and formed two countries—North and South Vietnam. The South Vietnamese government allied itself with the United States and other Western powers. But the government of North Vietnam, embittered by the split, wanted to take over the South and reunite the country—with a Communist government. So the North encouraged and supplied Communist Viet Cong rebels in the South. This action would evolve into a long guerrilla war against the new South Vietnamese government. By 1962 the

Viet Cong forces had grown so strong it looked like they might take over the South. So the United States had begun to send in American military advisors to train and strengthen the South Vietnamese army and support the weakening government of America's ally.

Soon after he arrived in Southeast Asia, Captain Colin Powell was assigned to a Vietnamese military unit in the A Shau Valley of South Vietnam. For weeks at a time, he and his unit patrolled the remote, rugged, and mountainous jungle region near the country's border with Laos, searching out Viet Cong guerrillas, their supply lines, and their strongholds.

Colin and his men carried everything they needed—food, water, clothes, weapons, ammunition—on their backs as they climbed up and down mountains, waded through jungle swamps, and swam across snake-infested rivers. The tropical heat often seemed unbearable, but Colin kept his long-sleeved shirts buttoned up and his camo pants tucked tight in his boots as protection against the knife-sharp blades of elephant grass and hordes of unpleasant jungle critters.

The unit's orders were to find and attack enemy forces, but Colin soon found that they were more often on the defensive. Snipers ambushed them almost every morning around dawn.

This was dangerous, difficult, and nerve-wracking warfare. Yet every day was the same. Marching through steaming jungles, searching for signs of the enemy, watching and waiting for unseen attackers who could open fire at any moment from any direction. They had to avoid land mines and booby traps, designed to kill or maim those who stepped on them.

One night, during a mortar attack on Colin's hilltop camp, a huge white flash exploded just twenty feet above his head. He dove to the ground and crawled into his bunker before another mortar round found him. But others had not been so fortunate. Hearing their shouts and moaning, Colin left his bunker to help the other men.

Not until the next morning did he see exactly what had happened. The mortar round had struck the branch of a tree he'd been standing under— scattering shrapnel to the right and left of him, wounding a half dozen men on either side. If the mortar hadn't hit the branch, it very probably would have killed him.

The day after that mortar attack, a helicopter hovered over the camp to drop supplies and a bag of mail. Soon Colin planted himself under a tree and opened a letter from his mother. After filling him in on an assortment of family news, his mother wrote, "Oh, by the way, we're absolutely thrilled about the baby."

That's how he learned that he was a father. Colin was beside himself with excitement, but he still didn't know if he had a son or a daughter. Was Alma all right? So he had his radio operator reach the base camp, where an earlier letter from Alma was sitting in a stack of undelivered mail. "Read it to me now," he said. And as he listened, he learned his wife had given birth to a son named Michael several weeks earlier.

Colin very much wished he could be with Alma and the baby. Instead, he was deep in the Vietnamese jungle suffering from diarrhea and attacks by mosquitoes and blood-sucking leeches that dropped on his head from the trees or wriggled underneath his clothing when he waded through water. And it would be six long months before he could make it home.

One day that summer, while leading a patrol out of enemy territory and back to a base camp to rest, Colin felt his right leg go out from under him and a sharp sting in his foot. When he looked down, he realized he had stepped into a simple Viet Cong booby trap consisting of a hole containing a punji stick—a sharp, poisoned bamboo spike. It had sliced through the sole of his jungle boot, entering the sole of his foot and poking out the top of his instep.

By the time he'd limped another two hours into camp, his foot was so swollen and purple that the medic had to cut his boot off. Colin was immediately evacuated by helicopter to a base hospital for surgery. He received a Purple Heart medal for his wound, which took several weeks to heal. Then

he finished the rest of his yearlong tour of duty in Vietnam.

When Colin arrived home, he was thrilled to see Alma and meet little Michael for the first time. But he was upset to learn about some of the things that had happened in his absence. While he was off fighting for the rights and freedoms of foreigners on the other side of the world, Alma had lived with her parents in Birmingham, where peaceful civil rights marchers had been viciously beaten and jailed. They had been protesting unfair laws that said black people couldn't eat in white restaurants, play on public playgrounds, or use the same water fountains white people used. The bombing of a Birmingham church had claimed the lives of four little black girls, creating a high level of racial tension. It had become so bad that some nights while Alma and her baby slept, her father sat up with a loaded shotgun, ready if necessary to defend his home and family against a mob.

Colin wasn't ready to join those who wanted to overthrow the government. But the unfairness and bigotry angered him. And when President John F. Kennedy, a supporter of civil rights for all Americans, was assassinated just a few weeks after his return, Colin Powell couldn't help but wonder about his country's future.

One day Colin drove into Buck's Barbecue, a fast-food restaurant in Columbus, Georgia, near where he was stationed at Fort Benning. When he

ordered a hamburger, the waitress asked if he were by chance an African student.

"No," he told her.

"A Puerto Rican?"

"No."

"You're a Negro then?" she asked.

When he told her he was, she informed him she couldn't bring him a hamburger out front, but if he would pull around, she would be glad to give him one at the back door.

As Colin backed out and drove away, he spotted the owner and some of his buddies through the restaurant window. They were still laughing as he angrily drove off down the street.

But things were slowly changing. The United States government soon passed laws making it illegal for restaurants in the South to refuse to serve black people. And after President Lyndon B. Johnson signed the Civil Rights Act of 1964, Colin made a point of returning to Buck's Barbecue.

Walking in the front door, he sat down at a nearby table and ordered a hamburger. He sat in the restaurant and ate it—then quietly walked out without saying a word to the owner.

9

IN VIETNAM AGAIN

Despite the turmoil going on in America, the next five years were some of the happiest of Colin Powell's life. He and Alma were together again, and he loved being a father to his son Mike and his daughter Linda, who was born in the spring of 1965.

Most of his time was spent in Georgia at Fort Benning, where he had a variety of duties. Colin did so well in the nine-month Infantry Officers Advanced Training course that he was promoted to major and selected to be an instructor at the school the next year. Later Colin was assigned to be a test officer for the U.S. Army's infantry board. All the equipment soldiers use—from weapons to boots to shovels to canteens—must be field tested to make sure they won't fail the men who depend on them in combat.

In between those assignments, Colin participated in the army's Pathfinder Course. Pathfinders are elite scouts who parachute into enemy territory ahead of airborne troops in order to mark landing and drop zones. The training was rough, and most of his classmates were experienced parachutists assigned to airborne units. They did exercises each morning until every man collapsed—then ran five miles. The rest of the day was spent attending classes. At night they practiced jumping out of airplanes when they couldn't see what dangers lay below.

Colin admitted later that daylight or darkness didn't matter much to him because he always closed his eyes when he jumped. In fact, he hated stepping out of a plane so much that instead of taking a bold leap like most of his classmates, he said, "I tended to shuffle to the rear and baby step off the ramp. As a result, while others soared like eagles, I managed to bang my butt on the ramp and bounce out of the plane." And yet on graduation day, he says, "To my surprise, this ground-loving soldier graduated number one in the class. I was proud of the honor, but I do not regret that I never again found myself in a situation where I had to jump out of an airplane."

While at Fort Benning, Major Colin Powell continued his training and participated in the training of other officers for combat duty in the jungles of Southeast Asia. The war in Vietnam continued and expanded until there were half a million American military personnel fighting on the other side of the world. So it seemed almost certain that Colin would have to leave his family for another yearlong tour of duty overseas. "You've got to be ready for it," he warned Alma. "It's going to happen."

But that day was postponed when Colin received word that he had been selected to attend the Army Command and General Staff College (CGSC) at Fort Leavenworth, Kansas. Instead of leaving his family and heading off to a war on the opposite side of the world, Colin loaded up his family and moved to Kansas.

Established in 1827 on the Missouri River, Fort Leavenworth is a historic military post on the edge of the western frontier. The first thing Colin did when he arrived was to search out a grassy, sunken lane that ran from the river up to the fort. He knew that the lane marked the spot where pioneers arriving by flatboat had unloaded their covered wagons and begun their journeys west toward the Santa Fe and Oregon Trails. He could practically feel the pulse of history on that spot. And every morning as he walked to class, he said, "I felt thrilled to be walking along roads that had known the footsteps of George Armstrong Custer, Philip Sheridan, Dwight Eisenhower, George Patton, and other storybook soldiers."

Most of his classmates at CGSC were older and more experienced majors and lieutenant colonels.

When Colin learned that many of them had earned graduate degrees while still in the service, he decided that applying for the army's Graduate Civil Schooling Program would be a good career move. He mentioned the idea to one of his superiors, but when the officer took a look at Colin's college record, he commented, "You don't look like graduate school material to me."

That reaction made Colin more determined than ever, and he set out to prove the officer wrong. By the time he finished second in his class at the Command and General Staff College the next year, there was little doubt that he would qualify for the army-sponsored graduate program. But the war was still on, so he first had to put his new classroom training to work on the battlefields of Vietnam.

By 1968 many Americans questioned their country's commitment to Vietnam and the wisdom of the war. It was difficult for military men to fight a foreign war without the respect and full support of people back home. But for Major Colin Powell, the toughest part of his second tour in Vietnam was leaving his young family for another year.

When he'd left Vietnam in 1963, there were only sixteen thousand Americans stationed in the country. When Colin landed in Saigon, South Vietnam's capital, in July 1968, GIs swarmed everywhere.

Upon his arrival, Colin was assigned as executive officer of an infantry battalion in the American Division. Colin handled a lot of the administrative duties and office work so his commander could concentrate on fighting the war. Such duty wasn't what he'd hoped for, but he worked hard and so inspired the people under him that the battalion scored the highest inspection ratings in the division.

The upper brass, however, noticed Colin as the result of a simple picture in the newspaper. One day the division commander, General Gettys, was reading a two-month-old copy of the *Army Times* newspaper when he noticed a photo of the top graduates in the most recent class of the Command and General Staff College at Fort Leavenworth. The general remembered meeting Colin when he arrived in Vietnam.

"I've got the number two Leavenworth graduate in my division, and he's stuck out in the boonies as a battalion exec? Get him up here," General Gettys ordered his aide. "I want him on my staff."

Almost overnight, Colin went from looking after the needs of an eight-hundred-man battalion to directing operations and planning warfare for nearly eighteen thousand troops, artillery units, aviation battalions, and 450 helicopters. It was an important and challenging job, and he was the only major in Vietnam trusted with the task. Every other operations and planning officer in the army was at least a lieutenant colonel.

Colin regularly traveled by jeep to meet with field officers and visit the troops in the surrounding jungle camp. But one day in November 1968, General Gettys, his chief of staff Colonel Treadwell, the general's aide Captain Tomelson, and Major Colin Powell all flew in the general's helicopter west of Quang Ngai to the site of a major American victory. The 11th Brigade had captured twenty-nine enemy base camps, a headquarters, a training post, and a large cache of weapons and enemy documents. A battalion commander had ordered his men to hack a landing site out of the jungle so the general's chopper could land. And they set off a smoke grenade to mark the spot and show the pilot which way the wind was blowing.

But the opening in the trees was so small the helicopter pilot missed on the first pass and had to come around a second time. As he hovered and slowly began to descend, pieces of chopped-up branches and leaves filled the air. Colin could see that there wasn't enough clearance for the chopper to safely land. He shouted to the pilot, "Pull out!" but it was too late. Just then one of the blades struck a tree trunk.

Colin later remembered, "One minute we were flying—the next, the helo dropped like an elevator with a snapped cable." He instinctively leaned over, put his head down, and wrapped his arms around his knees. After a three-story drop, the helicopter slammed to the jungle floor.

In training he'd been taught that survivors needed to get away from a crashed aircraft as quickly as possible—before it catches fire and explodes. So Colin unfastened his seat belt and jumped out the door, just behind the gunner. But the two men didn't get far from the wreck before they realized everyone else was still on board and not moving.

The gunner ran back to force open the pilot's door. Colin climbed back into the aircraft's hold, which was quickly filling with smoke from the still grinding engine. Colin found General Gettys, barely conscious with what looked like a broken shoulder. He released the officer's seat belt and dragged him away from the craft and into the trees. Several soldiers in the nearby jungle came running and went back to the helicopter with Colin. They located Colonel Treadway and hauled him to safety.

Returning to the smoking chopper a third time, Colin found the general's aide covered with blood and pinned in his seat between the radio and an engine that had smashed through the fuselage. Colin was sure the captain was dead. But when he pulled him free, the man moaned. Colin dragged him out of the burning craft before it exploded.

Only after everyone in the helicopter had been rescued did Colin stop to think about the pain in his foot. When all the survivors were evacuated by another helicopter back to the base hospital, x-rays revealed that Colin had suffered a broken ankle.

Usual policy was to send anyone with a broken bone to Japan, because Vietnam's dampness and humidity hindered healing. But Colin stayed to do his job and hobbled around for a week before the cast started crumbling. After that he used an Ace bandage. His doctors told him he was being foolish, and they were probably right. It took almost seven years for the ankle to completely heal and the pain to disappear when he stepped on it wrong.

By the time Major Colin Powell finished his second tour of duty in Vietnam, he was a well-respected and highly decorated officer with a second Purple Heart and a Legion of Merit. He was also awarded the Soldier's Medal for his actions after the helicopter crash. It is the U.S. Army's highest award for heroism in a noncombat situation.

Colin returned home from a war he knew would never be won to a country where there were no heroes' welcomes, no brass-band salutes, no victory parades. Very few people seemed to understand or appreciate the service he and other Vietnam veterans devoted to their country.

10

WORKING IN
WASHINGTON

Soon after Major Colin Powell returned to the States, he began graduate school at George Washington University in Washington, D.C. Although still officially part of the U.S. Army, the major lived more like a civilian while working on his masters of business administration (MBA). The Powells bought their first home across the Potomac River in Dade City, Virginia.

Colin was now thirty-two years old, and he felt a little out of place in classes where he was usually the oldest student. Although he'd excelled in all the military schooling he'd had since he joined the army, he remembered that he hadn't done nearly that well in college. He determined to do better this time. And he did.

Colin even surprised himself when he realized he had earned A's in all his first-semester classes. In fact he made A's in every one of his graduate-school classes—except one. He received a B in a course called Computer Logic.

Two important things happened in Colin Powell's life during his graduate school days. In the spring of 1970, Alma gave birth to their second daughter, Annemarie Powell. And that same summer, the major learned he was being promoted to lieutenant colonel. Since he was in school and there would be no formal promotion ceremony, Colin organized the family troops in the living room and had seven-year-old Michael pin a silver oak leaf (the insignia for a lieutenant colonel) on his sport shirt.

When he graduated with his MBA in 1971, the army assigned Lt. Colonel Powell to the Pentagon, the headquarters for all of the U.S. military forces. Colin was glad that his family wouldn't have to move again, since their Virginia home was only a few miles from the Pentagon. But he was a little worried about what kind of a job the army had in mind for him now that he had a graduate degree.

But instead of working with computers, which he wasn't excited about, Colin was assigned to the office of General William E. DuPuy, the assistant vice chief of staff for the U.S. Army. The general, whose job it was to make plans for the future of the army, had a reputation for being demanding and tough on his staff. But Colin had never shunned hard work. He and his new boss got along just fine. And he learned how the army worked at the highest levels in Washington.

Colin learned another very valuable lesson from General DuPuy. One day as they were traveling along together, the general gave him some advice. He said it was important for a man not to get so wrapped up in his career "that nothing is left that belongs only to you and your family." He urged Colin to build a strong personal and family life outside the military.

Colin would never forget what the general said—even though he was in some ways already following that advice. Not only was his family life important to him, his church was as well. Like his father before him, Colin attended church regularly and took time to serve as a leader at St. Margaret's Episcopal Church in Woodbridge, Virginia. He and Alma helped organize all sorts of church activities—from pancake suppers to the congregation's annual fundraising drive. Their children served as acolytes. And Colin even taught the fifth-grade Sunday school class.

The church and faith that had been so important as they grew up continued to be important to Colin and Alma Powell as adults. They made church life a central part of the family's values and tradition they passed along to their children.

During this time, the Powell family had to adjust to a civilian lifestyle. Not only were they living in a suburban home instead of military housing, but also the children now attended public schools instead of schools on the post. And Alma shopped in civilian stores instead of the PX.

Even as a lieutenant colonel, Colin didn't make the salary he would have made working at a civilian job. So the family didn't have a lot of money. They drove a rusty 1963 Chevy they had purchased from one of Alma's uncles for eighty-eight dollars. Alma hated to be seen in such a junker, so one weekend morning, Colin got up early, went to a nearby drug store, and bought a can of white latex house paint. Then he hurried home and went to work. When he woke up Alma a little while later to show her how he'd given the old car a new white paint job, she was thrilled. From a distance, the car looked almost new. Only if someone got within six feet could they see the brushstrokes.

One day while he was working for General DuPuy, a major from the infantry branch of the army called to say he was sending an eight-page application for Colin to fill out over the weekend. When he asked, "An application for what?" the officer said it was for a White House Fellowship. Colin indicated that he wasn't interested, but the officer informed him he didn't have a choice.

The White House Fellow program was created to expose impressive young leaders from all over the country to the highest levels of the federal government in Washington. Most of the participants came from academic institutions and private business; but the military had decided they wanted more representation. So Colin was ordered to apply.

More than 1,500 people applied. When Colin learned he was one of 130 who would be interviewed, his proud family was already talking as if he had the job. "Colin's goin' to the White House. Gonna help the president!" Thirty-five applicants were granted a final interview. And he was one of 17 selected—1 of 2 African-Americans picked for the program.

Colin was assigned to work as a special assistant for the year in the Office of Management and Budget (OMB), one of the most important government agencies in Washington. He worked closely with three of President Richard M. Nixon's appointees: Caspar Weinberger, Frank Carlucci, and Fred Malek. He worked on the White House grounds at the Executive Office Building, learned how the government worked, met a lot of important people, and even got to travel through the Soviet Union and China as part of the program.

At the end of his fellowship year, his bosses asked him to stay on as part of the Nixon administration. But Colin, who remained a military man at heart, wanted to get back to the army. So he turned down the offer and asked his superiors at the Pentagon for a command position.

He was offered command of the 1st Battalion, 32nd Infantry, 2nd Infantry Division, Eighth Army, Korea. The bad part was that Korea was what the army called an unaccompanied tour—he couldn't take his wife and family. He'd be gone for twelve months—leaving Alma alone in Virginia with three youngsters ages ten, eight, and three.

"I'm asking you to make quite a sacrifice," he admitted to Alma.

She had to agree. "But if this is what you think is best," she told him, "then do it."

He couldn't have done it without Alma's encouraging support. But having to leave his wife and family again was the most painful thing he'd ever had to do.

The battalion Lt. Colonel Powell commanded was based at Camp Casey, located just south of the demilitarized zone (DMZ). That was the term given to a neutral, noncombat area along the border separating North and South Korea.

When he arrived in Korea, the 1st Battalion had a terrible reputation for low morale, drug abuse, and racial tension. But the division commander, Major General Hank "Gunfighter" Emerson, thought Colin could bring the battalion under control. He supported Powell's crackdown on racial problems and drugs.

A little extra discipline made a huge difference. "I threw the bums out of the army and put the drug users in jail," he said. "The rest we ran four miles every morning, and by night they were too tired to get into trouble." By the time he finished his year's assignment in Korea, Colin had turned a rag-tag bunch of soldiers into a disciplined fighting force ready to take on any challenge. He did such a good job that General Emerson rated him as one of his top two (out of sixty-five) battalion commanders in all of Korea.

Colin gladly accepted another assignment at the Pentagon before receiving more training at the prestigious National War College at Fort McNair in Washington, D.C. One of the best things about both assignments was that it meant his family could continue to live in their house in Virginia.

Halfway through his time at the National War College, in February 1976, Colin was promoted to full colonel. And when he graduated later that year, he was one of two officers in his class given command of an infantry brigade. This time his family did have to move—to Fort Campbell, Kentucky.

After Colin completed his yearlong assignment, the family moved back to the Washington area. Colin was reassigned to the Pentagon and then asked to work for John Kester, who was an assistant to the secretary of defense during the Carter presidency.

Kester had read Powell's record—White House Fellowship, command and Pentagon experience, Vietnam War decorations, an MBA, a proven soldier—and he liked what he saw. "I checked you out," he told Colin during his interview. "And I've heard a lot of good things about you."

"And I checked you out," Powell told him. He grinned at Kester. "It wasn't all good."

Colin got the job. Some time later, President Carter's deputy director of defense, Charles Duncan, asked Powell to be his chief military assistant. Duncan said he liked three things about Colin Powell: He worked very well with people, he was a fast learner, and he had enormous energy and stamina. Evidently he wasn't the only person who noticed.

One evening while his mother was visiting, Colin asked everyone to gather around the table for a family meeting. Everyone wondered what was going on, but they all took their seats and waited to hear what he had to say.

He looked from one to another. Then he said, "I just wanted to tell you that today the president said I get to be a general." His mother hugged him. Alma and the children were thrilled.

When Ronald Reagan defeated Jimmy Carter in the 1980 presidential race, Colin thought maybe his Department of Defense days had come to an end. But when President Reagan appointed Caspar Weinberger and Frank Carlucci as his secretary and deputy secretary of defense, his former bosses from the Nixon administration asked General Powell to stay on as their chief military assistant.

Just the same, when he had the chance a few months later to return to the army and take a field command position, Colin jumped at the chance. First he went to Fort Carson in Colorado to be the assistant division commander for operations and training of the 4th Mechanized Infantry Division. Then he went to Fort Leavenworth as deputy commanding general.

After he earned his second star (making him a major general), Colin Powell was called back to Washington. The secretary of defense wanted him to serve as his chief military assistant. It was an important job that gave Colin an opportunity to meet some of the most important people in Washington, as well as top leaders from other countries. Still he wanted to get back to the army and the work he really loved.

In 1986 the secretary of defense agreed to let him leave to accept command of the U.S. Army's V Corps in Frankfurt, Germany. He was going back to the country where he'd begun his military career; this time he wasn't a new lieutenant guarding a border, but the commander of one hundred thousand men. And he also got his third star, making him a lieutenant general. Colin loved where he was and what he was doing so much that he said he was "probably the happiest general in the world."

Then he got a phone call from Washington. It was his old friend and former boss, Frank Carlucci, who had just been appointed national security advisor to President Reagan. "I need you to be my deputy," he said.

"I'm finally back in the real army," Colin told him and asked that he find someone else. "There's only one way I'll do it—if it's a direct request from the commander-in-chief."

A couple days later, the phone rang in the Powells' kitchen. It was President Reagan. He told Colin he knew how much he wanted to continue as commander of V Corps, but that it was crucial to the country for Colin to come home and help Frank Carlucci straighten out the National Security Council.

"I'll do it," General Powell said.

"God bless you," President Reagan told him.

And that's how Colin Powell came back to Washington to work in the West Wing of the White House for the rest of the Reagan administration. He did it not because it was a prestigious job, but because as a soldier, he felt compelled to fulfill the wishes of his commander-in-chief.

11

SOMEONE RIGHT FOR THE JOB

The Powells had been back in Washington only a few months when the general who had taken his place in Europe called one day with bad news about Lieutenant Mike Powell. Colin's son had followed in his father's footsteps, joining the ROTC while attending the College of William and Mary and then accepting a U.S. Army commission as a second lieutenant. Also, like his father, Mike was serving his first overseas tour of duty in Germany. Returning to the base one night, the driver of the jeep in which he was riding lost control. The vehicle rolled over, leaving Mike seriously injured.

Colin hurried home to tell Alma and wait for further news. She listened calmly but wanted to know how soon they could see their son. It wasn't long. President Reagan arranged for them to fly to Germany that evening aboard a military aircraft.

When they arrived at the U.S. Army hospital, Mike was receiving so many IV fluids and was so swollen that the Powells barely recognized their son. They learned he'd been thrown from the jeep, which then rolled over him. He had sustained a crushed pelvis, broken back, and massive internal injuries.

Mike's doctor told them, "His condition is critical. We don't expect him to live."

Colin and Alma told him they expected their son would live. "And we expect you to do everything you can for him."

While the doctors worked, the Powells prayed for their son. They soon arranged Mike's transfer to Walter Reed Army Hospital in Washington, D.C., where excellent doctors were able to perform an experimental surgery they hoped would help Mike recover.

Alma stayed with her son around the clock. Colin would spend as much time at the hospital as he could.

The Powells' prayers were answered. But recovery was slow and painful. Mike had fourteen surgeries over the next nine months. And when he was finally released from the hospital, the army gave him a full medical disability.

But one especially good thing came out of the tragedy. A young woman Mike had dated in college happened to be working in Washington at the time and heard about Mike's accident. She went to the hospital to see Mike and soon was visiting him every day. Seven months after his release from the hospital, Mike Powell and Jane Knott were married.

Mike did more than survive the accident. He learned to walk again, got married, became a father, and entered law school.

Despite all that was happening in his private life, Colin Powell's professional life was not slowing down. As deputy national security advisor, he regularly participated in meetings with the president, the vice president, and other cabinet members. He argued for strong language in a speech the president gave at the Brandenburg Gate along the Berlin Wall that same summer. The State Department wasn't so sure it was a good idea, but Reagan took the advice and said in the speech, "Mr. Gorbachev, open this gate . . . tear down this wall."

In the fall of 1987, when Frank Carlucci was named the new secretary of defense, the president appointed General Colin Powell as national security advisor. It was now his job to meet with the president almost every day, advise him on any foreign, domestic, or military matters that might affect the security of the nation, and head up the work of the National Security Council, which included the president, the vice president, and the secretaries of state and defense. It was the most powerful government position any African-American had ever held in our nation's history.

Almost overnight Colin became one of the most popular figures in the Reagan administration. He was in constant demand as a speaker, and his office was nearly overwhelmed with media interview requests. But his job kept him so busy that he had to turn down most of the invitations.

Over the last fourteen months of President Reagan's second term, Colin coordinated and directed three summit meetings with the Soviet's President Gorbachev as well as overseeing an economic summit of world leaders and friendly summits with Mexico, Canada, and NATO allies. And in addition to all this, Colin advised the president on a day-to-day basis.

When he appointed General Powell as his national security advisor, President Reagan said, "Sometimes you just know someone is right for the job. That's how I feel about Colin Powell."

Throughout the remainder of Reagan's presidency, Colin lived up to the president's faith in him. "Finding someone who will talk straight to you in Washington is a rare and valuable asset," Reagan said of his national security advisor. "But to find someone who is straightforward and loyal is invaluable."

One of Colin Powell's prized possessions is a photograph taken as he briefed President Reagan.

On the back, the president wrote, "If you say so, Colin, it must be right," and signed his name. Colin appreciated the confidence the president placed in him. But he also felt the heavy weight of responsibility because that level of trust, he admitted, "could be a little frightening."

Vice President George H. W. Bush, whose office was next to that of the national security advisor, also got an up-close look at Colin Powell's leadership style. He was so impressed that when he was elected president in 1988, he immediately asked Colin to stay on in his administration and offered him his choice of positions—heading up the Central Intelligence Agency (CIA) or becoming the second in command at the State Department. But Colin turned down both jobs, telling the new president he preferred to serve in the army again.

So in April 1989, Colin received another promotion, this time to four-star general. He was also appointed Commander-in-Chief of the Forces Command at Fort McPherson in Atlanta, Georgia. This meant he was responsible for seeing that one million active-duty army personnel, reservists, and National Guard personnel were trained and properly equipped to defend U.S. interests anywhere in the world.

But once again, his appointment was cut short. After just four months, President Bush called to say he wanted Colin to serve as chairman of the Joint Chiefs of Staff, the committee made up of the top officer in each of the military services—army, navy, air force, and marines. The president said when he announced the decision, "It is most important that the chairman ... be a person of breadth, judgment, experience, and total integrity. Colin Powell has all those qualities and more."

After more than three decades of service, General Colin Powell was officially the United States' highest-ranking military officer. Not only was he the principal person responsible for advising the president on all military matters, but also it was his job to see that the commander-in-chief's orders were then carried out by the military.

After reviewing the troops in a ceremony marking his new appointment, Colin gave a speech to a large group of the Pentagon's military and civilian employees. He wanted them to know how seriously he took his responsibilities. He described an enormous painting that he passed each day as he walked the halls of the Pentagon. It's an oil painting, done in the early 1960s by Woodi Ismael, depicting the inside of the Strategic Air Command Chapel. In the scene captured by the artist, bright sunlight streams through a stained-glass window, brightening the face of a man, his wife, and their children, as they kneel at the altar. The family is praying for the dad's safe return from war and that the family will have strength enough to face whatever happens.

"Every time I pass that painting," the new chairman said, "a silent prayer comes to mind for all of those who serve this nation in times of danger." Then he quoted the passage from Isaiah that is inscribed below the painting. "And the Lord God asked, 'Whom shall I send? Who will go for us?' And the reply came back, 'Here I am, send me.'"

Chairman Powell went on to say that America now had a historic opportunity to encourage a peaceful change from dictatorship to democracy in many countries around the world and that a strong military—ready to answer the call—would discourage aggression and encourage peace.

"And if we are successful," he concluded, "the men and women of our armed forces will pay only the price of eternal readiness and not the tragic and precious price of life."

Though he'd spent his adult life fighting, training, or planning for it, Colin Powell knew well the cost of war. This soldier who says that reading his favorite Bible passage (the "love chapter," 1 Corinthians 13) moves him deeply has always considered the use of force to be a last option. "War," he said, "should be 'the tool of last resort.'" To remind himself of that, Powell put a quote from Greek historian Thucydides beneath the glass cover of his desk in the Pentagon. It said: "Of all manifestations [or forms] of power, restraint impresses men most."

But on his second day in his new job, one of his generals called to say there was a problem brewing that might require military action. It was the first big challenge he would face as the United States' top soldier—but certainly not the last.

12

DEFEATING DICTATORS

Military officers in Panama were trying to overthrow their country's corrupt leader, General Manuel Noriega. The United States would have been glad to see Noriega leave office. For years he had pretended to be an ally while secretly cooperating with Latin American communists and making himself rich through deals with Colombian drug lords. He had been indicted in Florida for conspiring to smuggle drugs into the United States.

The leaders of the coup attempt requested U.S. military assistance. But they didn't seem organized enough to pull off their plan. And many American officials, including Colin Powell, remembering the mistakes made in Vietnam, hesitated to get involved in another country's internal problems.

When the coup failed and Noriega executed those who led it, Colin and others in the Bush administration were criticized by congressional leaders for not backing the dictator's opponents. But Colin continued to believe the president had done the right thing. He felt strongly that American forces should not be committed until there was a clear reason to do so and a well laid-out plan to follow.

On December 15, 1989, Noriega had his national assembly declare him Panama's "maximum leader" and then ratify a "state of war" with the United States. The following day, one of the members of the Joint Chiefs of Staff called Colin to say, "Mr. Chairman, we have a problem." Noriega's troops had fatally shot a U.S. marine and then abused the wife of a naval officer. President Bush and his advisors had run out of patience.

Colin led the planning meetings to develop a plan of attack. Early in the morning on December 20, 1989, the president of the United States announced the largest invasion conducted by American forces since the war in Vietnam.

This time the goal was clear—capture Noriega and destroy the elite forces loyal to him.

General Powell briefed the press on what was happening. Concern that the situation in Panama would turn into another Vietnam faded quickly as Noriega's forces were overcome in the first few days. Noriega went into hiding, but Chairman

Powell promised the American people that "we will chase him and we will find him."

General Noriega was trapped and surrendered before the end of the year. As he was hauled away to a federal prison in the United States, the people of Panama celebrated the end of his reign and the birth of democracy in their land.

Early in January Colin traveled to Panama to congratulate his troops and begin discussions on how and when to bring them home. He had been chairman of the Joint Chiefs of Staff for fewer than ninety days, but he'd overseen his nation's first major military encounter since Vietnam. The goal set by the military had been achieved with minimum American casualties. It was deemed an overwhelming success.

But the crisis in Panama turned out to be a warm-up for what was yet to come.

In August 1990 another dictator on the other side of the world challenged the United States and its allies. Hundreds of Iraqi tanks rolled over their border into the tiny neighboring country of Kuwait. Almost before the Kuwaitis knew what had happened, the Iraqi forces had taken complete control. Saddam Hussein, the Iraqi leader, was angry that Kuwait was producing so much oil that the prices stayed low and his country's oil profits were reduced. He also accused Kuwait of illegally pumping more than its share of oil from a field on the border between the two countries. His solution was to declare Kuwait to be Iraqi territory and tell Kuwait's people they could accept his rule or he would turn their land into a graveyard.

Almost every nation in the world condemned Hussein's actions. Colin and other American leaders worried that the Iraqi leader might not stop with Kuwait but would try to take control of the world's biggest oil fields in nearby Saudi Arabia as well.

The Saudis were worried. So were American leaders. They all believed something needed to be done to stop Saddam Hussein. But what?

Colin and his generals worked out a plan to defend the giant oil fields of Saudi Arabia and gave it the code name Desert Shield. President Bush announced that Iraq would not be allowed to annex Kuwait. And to show how serious he was, American troops were sent to help defend our allies and other American interests in the Persian Gulf. Within four weeks one hundred thousand U.S. troops had been transported to Saudi Arabia, and the first impressive stages of Desert Shield were in place.

The United States and other countries cut off trade with Iraq. And Saudi Arabia cut off the oil pipeline that transported Iraqi oil to the shipping ports in the Gulf. Everyone hoped that when Hussein realized that money and food supplies would soon run out in Iraq, he would back down and leave Kuwait—but it didn't happen.

In a meeting with the president and other leaders, Colin suggested that it might be time to demand that the Iraqis get out of Kuwait and go home. President Bush took his advice and told a joint session of Congress on September 19 that the United States "had drawn a line in the sand" at the Kuwaiti-Iraqi border, and it was time for the invaders to get out or face serious consequences.

About this same time, Colin decided that the United States wouldn't be able to maintain a huge army in the Arabian desert for an indefinite length of time. If they were going to avoid another long and costly war like Vietnam, there would need to be a daring and imaginative plan to defeat the Iraqis swiftly and surely.

A defensive war wouldn't do it. An offensive plan was needed. So Chairman Powell flew to Saudi Arabia in order to confer with General Norman Schwarzkopf, the field commander of all U.S. forces in the Gulf region. They began talking about what they would need in the way of men and weapons to defeat the five hundred thousand Iraqi soldiers occupying Kuwait.

The buildup continued. More American and allied troops flew into Saudi Arabia. More warships sailed into the Gulf.

In November the United Nations passed a resolution authorizing the use of force to expel Iraq from Kuwait if the invaders didn't withdraw by January 15. Hussein bragged that the Americans would suffer a terrible defeat if they attacked his army.

But in a televised news conference he knew Hussein would be watching, Chairman Powell warned the Iraqi dictator, "Don't try to scare us or threaten us. It won't work; it never has."

Just before Christmas, Colin flew to Saudi Arabia to visit American troops in the desert. As he shared a meal of cold chicken à la king squeezed out of a plastic tube, he told the men and women, "I know what it's like to be away from your family for the holidays. But this is important work. Stay with us. We'll take care of your families and get you home as fast as we can."

Back at home discussing strategy with the president, he advised: "Strike suddenly. Do it quickly, and do it with minimum loss of life."

When the January 15 deadline passed without any Iraqi movement, President Bush authorized the use of force. The next day, a massive air war began. On the first day, Allied planes flew three thousand missions, and thirty-three out of thirty-six Stealth missiles hit their targets. The allies lost only a handful of planes.

In a matter of days, the air war had crippled Iraqi military command and communication centers in Kuwait and Iraq. Food, ammunition, and other supplies were destroyed and supply lines cut off.

The plan was clear. Chairman Powell explained the strategy to one reporter by saying, "First we will cut off the Iraqi army, then we will kill it." His confident and impressive televised press conferences made him a nationally recognized hero.

Once the air war weakened the enemy, Generals Powell and Scwartzkopf had decided they would surprise the Iraqis by sweeping around their defensive positions on the Saudi border. Swinging around and behind them from the west would cut off any hope of retreat. On February 24 that's what the allied armies did. The strategy proved to be a brilliant success. In the first twenty-four hours, more than twenty-three thousand Iraqi troops threw down their weapons and surrendered.

On the second day of the ground war, Saddam Hussein ordered his troops to retreat from Kuwait City. But the allies had cut off their only route of retreat. By February 27 Kuwaiti troops had raised their nations flag once again over the capital in Kuwait City. And the day after that President Bush called for a ceasefire. Iraq surrendered unconditionally, and the war was over.

Many experts claimed it was one of the greatest military victories in history. Never before had so many troops been moved halfway around the world in such a short time. The strategy had been so good that an army of more than half a million men had been defeated in less than six weeks and with Allied casualties totaling fewer than a hundred killed.

Colin Powell was a bigger American hero than ever. But when he learned that a national magazine was planning to run his photo on the cover, he tried to talk the editors into putting General Schwartzkopf on the cover instead. And he told everyone who would listen that the real heroes of the war were the men and women on the front lines—his "kids," he proudly called them.

Despite the incredible success of the Gulf War, political popularity proved only temporary for President Bush. Just a year and a half after he declared the victorious liberation of Kuwait, George Bush lost his reelection bid to a young Arkansas governor by the name of Bill Clinton.

Many political experts said Bush would have been unbeatable if he had dropped Vice President Dan Quayle from the Republican ticket and made Colin Powell his running mate. The world will never know.

13

A RETIRED GENERAL

Colin Powell stood in his office in the Pentagon and looked around at the empty walls. He'd served the remaining nine months of his term as chairman of the Joint Chiefs of Staff under the new president. And on this day, he was retiring from the army. After today, he would no longer put on his uniform—no longer a general. He would be a retired general.

General Powell was surprised when he received word that President Bill Clinton wanted to see him. His official retirement ceremony was scheduled for four o'clock that afternoon, and the president planned to preside over the event. He had not expected to see the president before that time.

When Colin arrived at the White House, President Clinton invited him to sit on the Truman balcony, off the presidential living quarters. Colin sat in a lawn chair and the president in a rocking chair while they chatted. President Clinton told Colin that he was grateful for all he had done for his country. He asked if Colin would be willing to be the head of the president's Foreign Intelligence Advisory Board or the chairman of the D-Day fiftieth anniversary observances. Would he prefer to work with a national service program for young people? Colin told him that he did not want to do any of those things. Instead he wanted to write his autobiography and spend time with Alma and his family.

The two men discussed the U.S. military involvement in Somalia and other political and military problems for more than an hour.

When Colin returned to the Pentagon, he was surprised when former president George H. W. Bush dropped by to see him. After their visit, Colin went home to get Alma and dress for the official end of his military life.

People that Colin had known throughout his life were invited to attend his retirement ceremony. Looking around the parade grounds at Fort Meyers, he saw his sister Marilyn and her family, as well as some of his cousins. And he saw comrades from the Pershing Rifles, from Gelnhausen, Fort Devens, Vietnam, Fort Leavenworth, Fort

Carson, and Frankfurt. Church friends and White House Fellowship classmates were there. George and Barbara Bush, Vice President and Mrs. Al Gore, former vice president and Mrs. Dan Quayle, Dick Cheney, and many others were there to honor General Powell and his distinguished career.

There was one more surprise. Just before the ceremony began, a presidential aide told Colin that President Clinton planned to present him with the Presidential Medal of Freedom, the nation's highest, nonmilitary award.

Colin told the aide that he had already received that medal for his part in Desert Storm. But this, the aide said, was the Presidential Medal of Freedom, with Distinction. He showed Colin the medal that President Clinton would hang around his neck and a big, royal blue sash that would go around his waist.

"Not the sash," Colin said.

As the ceremony began, the sun came out from behind the clouds. Drums rolled, and the bugle corps played. Then cannons fired a nineteen-gun salute. The army band played a song written for the occasion: "Eye of the Storm: The General Colin L. Powell March."

The president hung the medal around Colin Powell's neck, but he didn't wrap the sash around his waist! Alma was given the army's Decoration for Distinguished Civilian Service.

Then President Clinton gave a speech in which he said, "I speak for the families who entrusted you with their sons and daughters ... you did well by them, as you did well by America."

General Powell looked out over the crowd and thought about his life: growing up in the South Bronx, ROTC at college, his days and nights in the jungles of Vietnam, the events that lead to Desert Storm—what it had been like to be responsible for more than two million soldiers, sailors, airmen, and marines. His military career had lasted for thirty-five years, three months, and twenty-one days.

After the ceremony, President Clinton had a present for General Powell. It was an old, rusty 1966 Volvo, ready for him to restore to running order. (For many years, restoring old Volvos has been one of Colin's hobbies.)

When General Powell spoke of his retirement, he said, "I had found something to do with my life that was honorable and useful, that I could do well, and that I loved doing. That is rare good fortune in anyone's life. My only regret was that I could not do it all over again."

The next morning, when Colin Powell came into the kitchen for breakfast, Alma told him, "The sink's stopped up. It's leaking all over the floor."

So former General Powell spent the first day of his retirement repairing the plumbing.

After Colin retired, most of his days consisted of ordinary civilian life. He spent time with Alma, their children, and their grandchildren. He worked on his old Volvo cars. He read books, watched movies, and continued to work on his autobiography.

But, every now and then, he and Alma would travel and do extraordinary things that only a retired four-star general and American hero could do.

In December 1993 Alma and Colin flew to London, where the queen of England knighted General Powell.

And in May 1994 Colin flew to South Africa to attend Nelson Mandela's presidential inauguration. Mandela was South Africa's first black president.

In September 1994 Colin Powell was asked to go with former president Jimmy Carter and Senator Sam Nunn on a peace mission to the island of Haiti. Together the three men persuaded Haitian leaders to sign an agreement that meant peace instead of war. Six hours after the papers were signed, U.S. troops landed to the cheers of the Haitian people.

Several months later Colin Powell was in his study when the telephone rang. A White House operator asked him to stand by for the president. President Clinton asked Colin Powell to stop by the White House the next day. He needed to talk to him.

Early the next morning, President Clinton told retired General Powell that Secretary of State

Warren Christopher was resigning. Would Colin be interested in the position?

General Powell told the president that he was honored to be asked but would have to say no. He was still writing his autobiography, and he and Alma wanted more time to enjoy their family. He had been out of the government affairs for little more than a year.

The president accepted his answer, and Colin left the White House shortly afterward. General Powell had no idea that he would ever be offered the position more than once.

On July 4, 1995, Colin Powell finished his autobiography. Just two months later, the book was in bookstores, and General Powell began his book tour. He started at a bookstore near his home in Virginia. Television crews were there to report on the event, and more than three thousand people came to buy the book and get Colin Powell's autograph. General Powell stayed for more than three hours, until every person had a signed book.

Then General Powell set out on a tour, talking about his book and his life. In five weeks he traveled to twenty-five American cities, England, and France. When he signed books in New York City, he was reunited with some of his childhood friends. When he went to Seattle, Washington, he was greeted by Bob Pyle, the gunner on the helicopter in which he had crashed in Vietnam.

At the end of the five weeks, General Powell had signed more than sixty thousand books and talked to countless people. Everywhere he went, people had asked if he were interested in becoming the next American president. He received many, many letters from people urging him to run. Some even felt that he had a duty to be president. This was a historic opportunity to elect the first African-American president.

But Colin Powell did not feel called to run for political office. He didn't have a full political agenda. And the thought of raising the millions of dollars he would have needed for a presidential campaign was unappealing to him. He asked friends if they thought he should run for president. He thought and prayed about the decision. He and Alma spent many hours talking about the possibility. Alma was emphatic—she did not want him to run.

Finally, on November 8, 1995, Colin Powell held a press conference and told the world, "I will not be a candidate for president or for any other elective office in 1996."

He explained how he had made his choice and how difficult the decision had been. And he concluded:

"Finally, let me say how honored I am that so many of you thought me worthy of your support. It says more about America than it says about me. In one generation, we have moved from denying a black man service at a lunch counter to elevating one to the highest military office in the nation and to being a serious contender for the presidency. This is a magnificent country and I am proud to be one of its sons."

14

AMERICA'S PROMISE

General Powell may not have wanted to run for president, but he still wanted to serve his country.

In April 1997 President Bill Clinton and former presidents George H. W. Bush, Jimmy Carter, and Gerald R. Ford, with former first lady Nancy Reagan, met in Philadelphia for what was called the Presidents Summit for America's Future. They challenged the nation to make five promises to the young people of America. Their Summit Declaration read:

> Our obligation, distinct and unmistakable, is to assure that all young Americans have
>
> • caring adults in their lives as parents, mentors, tutors, coaches.

- safe places with structured activities in which to learn and grow.
- healthy starts and healthy futures.
- an effective education to equip them with marketable skills.
- opportunities to give back to their communities through their own service.

Because those were five things he believed in, had benefited from, and believed the next generation needed to have, Colin Powell agreed to become the founding chairman of a new organization called America's Promise—a group made up of more than five hundred partner organizations devoted to fulfilling one or more of those promises.

America's Promise occupied a lot of Colin Powell's time for almost four years. But he saw it as another way to serve his country, making a difference in the lives of young people.

Everywhere he went, General Powell shared his experience and beliefs while speaking to adults and young people about working together for a better future and keeping America's promises.

In an interview for a magazine published by Prison Fellowship, the Christian ministry founded by former Nixon aide and Watergate conspirator Chuck Colson, General Powell had this to say to the 250,000 inmates who read *Inside Journal*.

"Despite your situation you can make something of your life; refuse to accept the view others have of you; attach yourself to something positive—family, church, or school. Take it slow but just stick to it; be your own person and make your own decisions; if you work hard and invest what is required to be successful you CAN make something of your life."

The interviewer in that article said, "Many young people are prisoners today because of the lure of easy money through drugs as opposed to hard work. A big part of your message is the value of work."

Everywhere he goes, General Powell tried to emphasize that point. "I don't know successful people who don't work hard," he said. "Success is hard work.

"Many interviewers come and sit with me and ask, 'Gee, how did you do it?' Worked like a dog— that's how I did it. I work very, very hard. I always have. I worked hard when I was mopping floors. I've worked hard since I was fifteen years old. I was never without a job. Most of the time it was pure manual labor while I was in high school and college.

"When I got out of college I joined the army, and I worked hard doing that for more than thirty years."

Hard work is a regular theme in Colin Powell's messages to young people. So are faith and belief.

He told people, "I believe in the country we live in; I believe in the system we have in this country; I believe in my family; I believe in myself;

and I believe in a God who gave us all life to use for a purpose."

General Powell thinks it's important to remember and build on the past. In a commencement speech at a mostly African-American college he told his audience:

"We must all reach back, we must all reach down. We must all work together to pull our people, to pull all Americans out of the violence, out of the dank and soul-damning world of drugs, out of the turmoil in our cities. As we climb on the backs of others, so must we allow our backs to be used for others to go higher than we have. . . . The other evening Alma and I were privileged to be with the poet Maya Angelou. She talked about her upbringing in Stamps, Arkansas. She told us something her grandmother had said to her many years ago. Her grandmother had told her, 'Girl, when you cross this threshold, you're gonna be raised.' So raise your children. Treasure them. Love them. They are our future. We cannot let the generation in front of us go to waste.

"So raise strong families, and as you raise your families, remember the worst kind of poverty is not economic poverty, it is the poverty of values. It is the poverty of caring. It is the poverty of love."

Colin Powell never forgot the love and caring he received growing up. He never forgot the opportunities he was given to learn and to achieve his dreams and promise. So when he was invited back to visit and speak in his old New York City neighborhood, many memories flooded his mind as he walked up the familiar, worn, stone steps of Morris High School. As he looked around at the mostly Hispanic and African-American faces of the students, he told them:

"I remember this place. I remember the feeling that you can't make it. But you can. When I was coming up, the opportunities were limited. But now they are there. You can be anything you want to be. But wanting to be is not enough. Dreaming about it isn't enough. You've got to study for it, work for it, fight for it with all your heart and soul."

He went on to point out that today more than 97 percent of GIs are high school graduates. "So don't drop out. Stick with it. I'm giving you an order: Stick with it. Stay in high school and get your diploma. Don't do drugs ... it's stupid. ... And don't think you're limited by your background. Challenges are there to be knocked down."

He also challenged kids to pick role models. "And feel free to choose a black or a white one, a general or a teacher, or just the parents who brought you into this world."

In his autobiography Colin Powell explained that he encourages young people to pick their role models from any race. "I'm concerned that the admirable ideal of black pride can be carried to an extreme where it produces isolation. ... I want black youngsters to learn about black writers, poets, musicians, scientists, and artists and about the culture and history of Africa. At the same time, we have to accept that black children in America are not going to have to make their way in an African world. Along with their black heritage, they should know about the Greek origins of our democracy, the British origins of our judicial system, and the contributions of our national tapestry of Americans of all kinds and colors. My message to young African-Americans is to learn to live where you are and not where you might have been born three centuries ago. The cultural gap is too wide, the time past too long gone, for Africa to provide the only nourishment to the soul or mind of African-Americans. The corollary is equally true. Young whites will not be living in an all-white world. They must be taught to appreciate the struggle of minorities to achieve their birthright."

He goes on to say, "I have lived and risen in a white-dominated society and a white-dominated profession, but not by denying my race, not by seeing it as a chain holding me back or an obstacle to be overcome. Others may use my race against me, but I will never use it against myself. My blackness has been a source of pride, strength, and inspiration, and so has my being an American. I started out believing in an America where anyone, given equal opportunity, can succeed through hard work and faith. I still believe in that America."

That belief in the future of America is why Colin Powell devoted his retirement years to working to help this country's young people through America's Promise. It is also why, in 2001, when President George W. Bush asked him to serve his country again, this time as its first African-American secretary of state, he accepted the assignment.

But no one could have imagined just how valuable he would soon be, forging an international coalition against terrorism after the attack on September 11, 2001, when hijackers flew two jetliners into the World Trade Center towers in New York, another into the Pentagon in Washington, D.C., and crashed a third plane in Pennsylvania. God had clearly prepared him for the most important role of his career. And Secretary of State Colin Powell knew there was more work to be done.

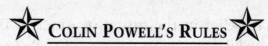

COLIN POWELL'S RULES

Here is a list of guidelines and lessons Colin Powell has learned over a lifetime. He keeps these basic principles handy to remind himself what it takes to achieve success in any task he undertakes.

★1.   It ain't as bad as you think. It will look better in the morning.

★2.   Get mad, then get over it.

★3.   Avoid having your ego so close to your position that when your position falls, your ego goes with it.

★4.   It can be done!

★5.   Be careful what you choose.
       You may get it.

★6.   Don't let adverse facts stand in the
       way of a good decision.

★7.   You can't make someone else's choices. You shouldn't let someone else
       make yours.

★8.   Check small things.

★9.   Share credit.

★10. Remain calm. Be kind.

★11. Have a vision. Be demanding

★12. Don't take counsel of your fears
       or naysayers.

★13. Perpetual optimism is a force multiplier.

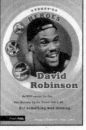

We want to hear from you. Please send your comments about this book to us in care of the address below. Thank you.

Zonder**kidz**™

Grand Rapids, MI 49530
www.zonderkidz.com